BAPTISM in Water & The Spirit

(Revised Edition)

BAPTISM in Water & The Spirit

(Revised Edition)

Brian Winslade

Oikos Books
Private Bag 3120, Waikato Mail Centre, Hamilton 3240, NZ

© Copyright 2019 Brian N. Winslade

(Formerly published 1995 and 2008 — ISBN 978-0-473-09265-8)

Brian N. Winslade asserts his moral right to be identified as the author of this work.

ISBN 978-0-473-47239-9

All rights reserved. No part of this publication may be produced or transmitted in any form or by any means, electronic or mechanical, including photocopying, recording or information storage and retrieval systems, without permission in writing from the copyright holder.

Cover Design by Luke Winslade
(luke.winslade@gmail.com)

Published by Oikos Books

Unless stated otherwise, all Scripture quotations in this book are taken from the HOLY BIBLE, NEW INTERNATIONAL VERSION. Copyright 1973, 1978, 1984 International Bible Society. Used by permission of Zondervan Bible Publishers

By the same author:

Shifting the Paradigms of The Normal Christian Church (1994)

Lord of All (Oikos Books, 2002)

A New Kind of Baptist Church – Reframing Congregational Government for the 21st Century (Morling Press, 2010)

They Want Me to be an Elder – What do They Do? (Oikos Books, 2018)

Boundaries – Rediscovering the Ten Commandments for the Twenty-First Century (Resource Publications, 2018)

Contents

Preface 9

Part One
1. Believers' Baptism 19

Part Two
2. The Person & Work of The Holy Spirit 45

3. Baptism in the Holy Spirit 59

4. How Can I Be Baptised in the Holy Spirit? 75

Preface

Imagine what it must have been like on the Day of Pentecost. Jerusalem was crowded with pilgrims from all over the Roman Empire who had come for the annual Feast of Weeks celebrations, and there was a festival atmosphere. The turmoil and confusion surrounding the execution of the radical Galilean some weeks back had largely abated. His followers still met together often, to pray and swap stories of how they had seen him resurrected, but few people took much notice of them any more. Most people who had been excited by Jesus had drifted back into anonymity.

Then it happened! From the windows of a second story room there came this strange sound - the sound of rushing wind, a ferocious gale. And then the sound of laughing and shouting. Minutes later a group of bewildered people spilled out into the streets. They looked drunk, totally overcome by some kind of drug. But then an even stranger thing started to happen: several of them started shouting sentence after sentence in languages they had never studied. Pilgrim Jews from different parts of the empire stood still to listen. They could hear people speaking in their native tongues - not in the international trade language they had learned, but in the language of the local people in their home country. And what was it they were hearing? It wasn't empty words, but a discourse about God and the wonders he had performed in the world.

This strange phenomenon must have gone on for some time, as a large crowd started to gather to see the spectacle. Nothing like this had ever happened before. Here were men and women who were uneducated; many of them illiterate. Yet they were speaking fluently in languages they themselves had never heard before. Perhaps no one was more surprised about what was happening than the very people through whom it was happening! As the crowd grew and grew, it became obvious that some kind of explanation was called for. In the confusion and general misunderstanding, those who were speaking in these foreign tongues were being accused of drunkenness!

Then Peter, with the other eleven Apostles, stood up to face the crowd. No doubt they had conferred with each other over what was happening and determined that this must be the coming of the Holy Spirit upon them - as their leader Jesus had predicted. He had told them to wait in Jerusalem for it to happen, and he'd even hinted that it would resemble the sound of a wind. But he'd not said anything about the huge commotion it would cause! Now there were thousands of people standing around them. The whole city of Jerusalem had come to a standstill. People wanted to know what was going on.

Then something happened within Peter. The man who a few weeks earlier had been a coward suddenly felt a boldness surge through him. He wasn't too sure just what he was going to say, but he was on his feet and motioning to the crowd to be still and listen. And as he began to speak he felt carried along - the words just flowed. He spoke to the crowd about Jesus of Nazareth, and who he really was—this man they had put to death during the previous Passover Festival. He told them how he fulfilled all the prophetic predictions about the expected

Messiah.

For some time Peter preached, and the crowds listened in stillness. What Peter was saying seemed to make sense. The commotion of the morning, coupled with the strange things that had been happening in Israel over the last three years, all seemed to point to the same conclusion. As people listened there was a stirring in the hearts of many. People were realising their complicity in the execution of Jesus of Nazareth. Perhaps there were many in the Pentecost crowd who had earlier stood in the mob outside Pilate's palace, calling for Jesus' blood. Whatever it was, there was a powerful anointing over that crowd of people who listened to Peter's discourse. They knew they were not in a right relationship with their God, and they wanted to do something about it. This is how Luke records what happened next:

> [37] *When the people heard this, they were cut to the heart and said to Peter and the other apostles, "Brothers, what shall we do?"*
> [38] *Peter replied, "Repent and be baptized, every one of you, in the name of Jesus Christ for the forgiveness of your sins. And you will receive the gift of the Holy Spirit.* [39] *The promise is for you and your children and for all who are far off—for all whom the Lord our God will call."*
> [40] *With many other words he warned them; and he pleaded with them, "Save yourselves from this corrupt generation."* [41] *Those who accepted his message were baptized, and about three thousand were added to their number that day.*
> *The Fellowship of the Believers*
> [42] *They devoted themselves to the apostles' teaching and to fellowship, to the breaking of bread and to prayer.*
>
> *Acts 2:37-42*

Neither the pages of history, nor even the record of Scripture, can ever adequately capture the amazing spectacle of the Day of Pentecost. The promised Holy Spirit burst forth onto the initial band of disciples, and the Christian Church was born. The ministry of Jesus had not ended, as the authorities might have hoped. The reverse was true - its full impact was really only just beginning.

There is a lot that has been written about the manifestation of Holy Spirit power on the Day of Pentecost, and rightly so. He, after all, was the star player. But the significance of the words Peter offered to those who wanted to respond to his message has, perhaps, been undervalued.

For instance, it has been suggested that the advice Peter gave here is the closest thing we have in the New Testament to a description of what a person needs to do in order to become a Christian. Peter was addressing a group of people who were under conviction by the Holy Spirit. They had recognised their need for forgiveness, and they wanted to correct their relationship with God. Peter's words had got through to their hearts, and they asked him what they should do.

Now, when someone asks the question, "What should I do in order to get my relationship with God put to right?" surely you answer them simply and precisely. When that kind of question is asked it is hardly the time for a lengthy and detailed theological lecture. You simply tell the basic rudiments of conversion.

That is what Peter did to the crowd who gathered on the Day of Pentecost. They asked what they should do, and Peter told them the basics of the conversion process. It is interesting to compare what Peter said with what most evangelists declare today. Having worked for an evangelistic organization, the typical evangelistic appeal today stresses belief in Jesus (and his atoning work on the cross) and submitting one's life to his Lordship (or management). There is, of course, nothing wrong with this advice, but Peter went considerably further. Conversion to Christ, according to Peter, was not merely an inward personal decision, but also an outward dramatic declaration, and a power encounter with the Holy Spirit.

There are at least four steps Peter suggested to those who wanted to get their lives right with God on the Day of Pentecost. The first step Peter spoke of was **repentance** - turning away from a life of sinful pleasure and choosing to follow Jesus. To become a Christian means a dramatic change in our ambitions and behaviour, not merely in our belief systems; which is why we often use the word *conversion* (meaning change).

But then Peter went a step further than most interdenominational evangelists. He suggested a second step was **baptism** in water, as a public declaration of faith in Christ. This was something he proposed for all those turning to Christ, which would, in turn, lead to a third step—being *filled with the Holy Spirit* (or baptism in the Holy Spirit, as Jesus had referred to it). Those who repented and were baptised would experience an encounter with the Holy Spirit and be empowered in a similar way to those on the Day of Pentecost.

The fourth part in the conversion process is more implicit, but none the less significant. Those who responded to his message were **added to the church**. We're not told exactly what Peter said about this, but clearly, something was communicated. Those who turned to Christ were numbered amongst the community of believers, later to be known as Christians. Following Jesus was not something they did in secret or isolation. A disciple of Jesus was part of a community of people who loved and nurtured one another in the faith.

The book you hold seeks to set forth a theological position for the second and third of Peter's steps in conversion. Baptism in water and in the Holy Spirit are initial steps in faith for the new Christian. Over the centuries some of their significance has been lost in the Christian church, and in some cases even denied as valid for today.

There are three groups of people in mind in the writing of this short book. Firstly, those who are new members of the family of God. Perhaps you have only recently become a follower of Jesus - *this book is for you* as an encouragement toward some of the early steps of obedience and empowering you might like to consider. You will no doubt want to read it and discuss it with someone further on in the spiritual journey, like your pastor or a trusted leader in your church.

Secondly, some reading this book may have been Christians for many years but have never been exposed to biblical exposition on believer's baptism. You have a profound love for Jesus, but the church tradition you have grown up with has not stressed the importance or significance of believers' baptism by immersion. *This book is for you* - as a challenge to obey one of the foundational commands of Christ and seeks to set forth as simply as possible the meaning of baptism, and why all Christians should participate in it.

Thirdly, there are some reading this book who may have been confused or concerned (perhaps even hostile) toward what some call the charismatic renewal that has swept through many Christian church communities in recent decades. Talk of baptism in the Holy Spirit, and gifts of the Spirit, seems foreign and unsettling. *This book is for you* - as an attempt to lay a sound theological foundation for what the Holy Spirit still does in the lives of believers. Many people who have been Christians for decades have testified to a profound sense of spiritual renewal through praying, or being prayed for, to be filled with the Spirit. God has touched them and changed them, and their experience of God's power bears similarity to that of the New Testament Church.

In God's economy, baptism in water and the Holy Spirit belong together. While they may happen at different times for some Christians, it was God's intention that they went hand in hand. And with these sacraments, a new convert is also enfolded into the fellowship of a caring community of faith. If this book helps any toward that end, its' objective will have been achieved.

To God be the Glory!

Brian Winslade
New Zealand
2019

Part One

One

Believers' Baptism

Evangelical Christians have a high view of the Bible and regard it is our authority for all we believe and practice in the Church. We often refer to it colloquially as the word of God and our foundation for understanding God and ourselves in response. If ever there is a conflict between what we say or do and what the Bible teaches, the evangelical assumption is that the Bible is right, and we need to change. The Scriptures are our primary revelation of God's will for us, and how we should conduct ourselves.

Accordingly, our convictions and practice on the subject of baptism are based simply on what we read of it in the Bible. Many people have made the sacrament of baptism into something convoluted and complicated, yet its original intent was actually a simple step of initiation into the family of God. Its meaning or significance is not at all hard to grasp.

To demonstrate, in this chapter we pose, and then answer, five questions about baptism in water:
1. What does the word "baptism" actually mean?

2. How important is baptism?
3. When should baptism take place?
4. What is the relationship between baptism and belonging to a church family?
5. What about those who have been Christians for many years, but have never been baptised?

1. What does the word "baptism" actually mean?

The English word baptism (or baptise) comes from the Greek word ***baptizo***, meaning literally to *dip, plunge, submerge* or *immerse*. It described the action of submerging or totally immersing something in a substance. The Christian concept of baptism practised over the last 2000 years, stems back to the time of the New Testament where converts would be ***baptizo*** in rivers or pools or in the sea. However, the actual idea of baptism stretches back to before the time of Jesus and the Christian church.

In Jewish religion and culture there existed a form of baptism that a proselyte (new convert to the Jewish faith) would go through in the presence of several elders. It was a form of initiation and ritualistic cleansing of past sins:

> *The Gentile entered the Jewish faith by baptism. The ritual was as follows. The person to be baptised cut his nails and hair; he undressed completely; the baptismal bath must contain at least forty seahs, that is two hogsheads, of water; every part of his body must be touched by the water. As he was in the water, he made confession of his faith before three fathers of baptism and certain exhortations and benedictions were addressed to him. The effect of this baptism was held to be complete regeneration; he was called*

a little child just born, the child of one day. All his sins were remitted because God could not punish sins committed before he was born. The completeness of the change was seen in the fact that certain Rabbis held that a man's child born after baptism was his first-born, even if he had older children . . .[1]

In the New Testament, baptism takes on a very important meaning, and no doubt borrows much of its theological symbolism from its Jewish roots. In essence, the action of being baptised is the physical enactment of the inward spiritual transformation that takes place (or at least began) at the time a person converts to Christian faith. The act of going into a pool of water and allowing oneself to be dipped or immersed is the acting out of a mini-drama, a symbolic declaration of something that has taken place in one's life. In theological terms, the '*something that has taken place*' is the death to an old way of living, and the beginning of a brand-new life within us. When a person becomes a Christian, we say that their old life has died or ceased, and a new life has begun. The Apostle Paul described it as a new beginning:

[17] Therefore, if anyone is in Christ, the new creation has come: The old has gone, the new is here!
2 Corinthians 5:17

The old life where we were boss or the controller of our destiny has been terminated, and a new life where Jesus is Lord has commenced. The act of baptism is a mini-dramatic-presentation of that fact.

Burial & Bath

Two symbolic metaphors are used in the New Testament to describe

---

[1] William Barclay, *"The Daily Study Bible - The Letter To The Romans"*, (The Saint Andrews Press, 1975), p.84.

baptism: a *burial* and a *bath*. In Paul's letter to the Christians in Rome, he likened the act of baptism to the burying of one's old life or nature with Jesus in the same tomb he was buried in after his crucifixion.

> [3] Or don't you know that all of us who were baptized into Christ Jesus were baptized into his death? [4] We were therefore buried with him through baptism into death in order that, just as Christ was raised from the dead through the glory of the Father, we too may live a new life.
>
> Romans 6:3-4

Just as Jesus was raised from the dead on the third day after he died, so the person being baptised declares that the Spirit of God has given them new life also. As a person comes up out of the water, they identify with the resurrection life of Jesus. Baptism is an enactment of the *death* and *resurrection* that takes place when a person surrenders leadership of their life to Jesus—the old life has died and was buried, and a brand-new life in Christ has begun.

As for the metaphor of a bath, in Acts 22 Paul was re-telling the testimony of how he came to faith in Christ, and how a man named Ananias was sent to him to heal his blindness. After Paul received his sight Ananias said these words to Paul:

> [16] And now what are you waiting for? Get up, be baptised and wash your sins away, calling on his name.
>
> Acts 22:16

Paul was speaking to Jews in Jerusalem on this occasion, and he likened the idea of baptism to the symbolic washing away of past sin—a concept they understood well. When a person becomes a follower of Jesus they are cleansed from their past sin, and the action of baptism symbolises this fact.

Mode of Baptism

When we note the theological symbolism of baptism, along with the meaning of the actual word, it gives a clear definition of the appropriate *mode* of baptism. Leaving aside for the moment the issue of infant baptism (which is discussed later), the majority of churches around our world have traditionally baptised by the sprinkling or pouring of water on the head, as opposed to full immersion. Many a theologian has argued at length as to whether the mode of baptism is really that important.

Given that many of our arguments over theology are seldom as important to God as we like to make them, it can be argued that the mode of baptism is important, and the Scriptures are very clear. Perhaps the matter only becomes complicated when attempts are made to defend a position that the Bible doesn't explicitly teach. Here are three reasons for total immersion as the valid form of baptism in water:

i. The meaning of the original word *baptizo*. It does not mean to wet or to sprinkle; a person cannot be immersed or submerged with a few drops of water. Indeed, it has been suggested that John 3:23 informs how much water is necessary in order to be baptised: John the Baptist chose the location of Aenon near Salim *"because there was plenty of water . . ."*

ii. The act of baptism symbolises the going into a grave. As a person is submerged in water it represents a dramatic presentation of the burial of a dead person and resurrection to new life. (We might say that it is done with water, rather than soil, so that people do live through the experience!). If baptism has a biblical and theological foundation, it is argued, how can this be adequately represented by a few drops of water?

iii. The New Testament Church clearly practiced baptism by immersion. The imagery and example of Christian baptism, adapted from its Jewish proselyte roots, is clear. If that was the way the first generations of the Christian Church understood the teaching of Jesus, what justification is there for adopting a different practice today?

Consequently, it is argued, to tamper with the mode of baptism is to disregard the meaning of words used in Scripture; saying that what they mean is unimportant. If we do that with a word like *baptism*, where else might we do it too? What is to stop us from changing the meaning of words like *repentance* or *salvation* or *forgiveness* or *judgment*? The clear meaning and mode of baptism in the New Testament is by total immersion in water; why should we do anything different?

2. How Important Is Baptism?

We've established what it means and symbolises, but is it an essential practice? Obviously, there are divergent opinions amongst different church traditions. The vast majority of Christian traditions actually argue that baptism is essential in order to be a part of the church and view it as a requisite means of entry. They might question the mode of baptism as outlined above, and when it ought to take place, but the importance of baptism is never challenged.

Then there are some churches that take an extreme view and contend that a person cannot be fully saved until or unless they are baptised, and that the mode must be by immersion. On the other hand, some churches and Christian ministries (e.g. Salvation Army) are more nonchalant about any form of church sacraments, such as baptism and communion, and practice or encourage neither. They argue that one doesn't have to be physically baptised in water in order to be saved and to be a part of the family of God.

And surely, they are quite right. Salvation is a matter of personal faith in Jesus, not in rituals or outward actions that depend upon human activity. Yet many still argue from the teaching of the New Testament that water baptism is important for all Christians and is a command of Jesus to be obeyed.

In at least two of Jesus' commissioning statements to his disciples, prior to his ascension into heaven, he mentions the command of baptism:

> [19] *Therefore go and make disciples of all nations, baptizing them in the name of the Father and of the Son and of the Holy Spirit,* [20] *and teaching them to obey everything I have commanded you. And surely I am with you always, to the very end of the age."*
> Matthew 28: 19 -20

> [15] *. . . Go into all the world and preach the gospel to all creation.* [16] *Whoever believes and is baptized will be saved, but whoever does not believe will be condemned.*
> Mark 16:15-16

New converts to the Christian faith, who believe the message of the gospel and accept Jesus as their Lord and Saviour, were to be baptised in water as a declaration of that fact.

In Matthew 3 we read Jesus' own example in regard to baptism. Like many people of his day, Jesus went out to where John the Baptist was baptising people as a symbolic act of repentance and turning to God. John recognised who it was approaching him:

> [13] *Then Jesus came from Galilee to the Jordan to be baptized by John.* [14] *But John tried to deter him, saying, "I need to be baptized by you, and do you come to me?"*
> [15] *Jesus replied, "Let it be so now; it is proper for us to do this to fulfill all righteousness." Then John consented.*
> Matthew 3: 13-15

From the very mouth of Jesus, baptism in water is presented as a means of *"fulfilling all righteousness."* Some have questioned the point of Jesus' baptism by John, given there was nothing for him to repent of, yet he presents the act of baptism is doing what is *right* before God. Therefore, those who submit to believers' baptism are doing nothing less than following the example or role model that Jesus has set.

Initiation into community

The overwhelming example throughout the New Testament depicts baptism as an act of initiation and acceptance into the company of people called Christians. This point is elaborated upon a little further on, but for now, let's note at least two statements that Paul makes that describe baptism as a way of joining or being added to Christ and the Church:

> [12] *Just as a body, though one, has many parts, but all its many parts form one body, so it is with Christ.* [13] *For we were all baptized by one Spirit so as to form one body—whether Jews or Gentiles, slave or free—and we were all given the one Spirit to drink.*
> 1 Corinthians 12:12,13

> [26] *So in Christ Jesus you are all children of God through faith,* [27] *for all of you who were baptized into Christ have clothed yourselves with Christ.*
> Galatians 3:26,27

The act of baptism was interpreted by the first Christians as a public declaration of new-found faith in Christ. It was a public drama or enactment of the faith one had come to. It was most likely the declaratory statement of baptism that Paul wrote about to Timothy at the end of his first letter:

12 Fight the good fight of the faith. Take hold of the eternal life to which you were called when you made your good confession in the presence of many witnesses.
1 Timothy 6:12

When we read through the book of Acts there are numerous instances where new converts were baptised in this sense of public declaration and initiation. Chapter 2 tells the story of the dramatic outpouring of the Holy Spirit on the Day of Pentecost. V.41 tells us that on that day there were three thousand people who came to faith in Christ and declared this fact through baptism in water.

Chapter 8 tells the story of Philip the evangelist having been told by an angel to walk along a deserted road, only to meet up with a God-seeking Ethiopian treasury official, who invited Philip to travel with him (and his entourage) in his chariot. After hearing the good news of Christ and determining in his heart that he wanted to become a follower of Jesus, the Ethiopian's chariot came upon some water. They stopped, got down into the water, and Philip baptised him in the presence of all those travelling with him—a public testimony to his new-found faith in Christ.

Chapter 9 records the dramatic conversion of Saul, later to be known as Paul the Apostle. En route to Damascus in order to arrest and persecute Christians, Saul found himself arrested by the Lord. A great light blinded him, and he was led into Damascus where he remained blind for three days. As we've noted, the Lord sent a believer named Ananias to lay hands on him and heal him. Saul accepted Christ and was immediately baptised.

In Chapter 10 we read of the first gospel mission among Gentiles. A Roman centurion named Cornelius invited the Apostle Peter to come and share the good news of Jesus with him. When Peter arrived, he found Cornelius had invited a whole lot of his friends to hear what he had to say. Before Peter had finished talking the Holy Spirit came upon the gathering in power, and they started speaking in tongues—as on the Day of Pentecost. This is how Peter responded:

> [47] *"Surely no one can stand in the way of their being baptized with water. They have received the Holy Spirit just as we have."* [48] *So he ordered that they be baptized in the name of Jesus Christ. Then they asked Peter to stay with them for a few days.*
>
> Acts 10:47,48

In Chapter 16 we have two instances of people (or groups of people) hearing the good news, responding to Christ, and being baptised. First was a woman named Lydia who heard Paul and Silas' preaching. The Lord opened her heart to receive the truth, and immediately she and her entire household were baptised. Later on, Paul and Silas found themselves in jail on account of their ministry. The jail was securely locked, and Paul and Silas placed under heavy guard. Around midnight an earthquake shook the jail to its very foundations and all the doors flung open and the prisoners' chains fell off. The jailer woke and saw the doors open. Assuming the worst, he was about to commit suicide, when Paul called out to him. Paul shared with him about Jesus, and the jailer determined to become a Christian. He and his household (in the middle of the night!) were baptised as a statement of their faith in Christ.

When we read the New Testament and let it speak for itself, baptism in water does not ever appear to be presented as an optional extra for those Christians who want to take it up. The theology and practice of the early Church, with respect to baptism, seems to indicate that they regarded it as a command. How important is baptism? From the days of the earliest converts, it was clearly set forth as an outward declaratory statement of inner forgiveness and cleansing from sin. Jesus, Peter, Paul, Philip, Ananias (among others) all presented it as a definitive command and one which the early converts to Christianity willingly obeyed.

Can a person be a Christian and not be baptised? The answer, of course, would have to be *yes*. There are many followers of Jesus who have never been presented with the teaching or option of baptism, and there are others who struggle against it for a variety of reasons. It is not for us to judge the righteousness of others. Perhaps a better question to ask though is whether refusal or deferral of baptism is something that pleases the heart of God? From reading the New Testament it is clear that baptism was not man's idea, but God's! Holding back on baptism, therefore, is not an argument against the Church or historical tradition; it's an argument against Jesus. Baptism was his example and his command to those who would carry on the work he began.

3. When should Baptism take place?

Throughout the history of the Christian Church, certainly from the fourth century onwards, many Christian denominations have cited the timing of baptism as being for newborn infants. Little babies of Christian families are presented before the Church and baptised by the sprinkling or pouring of water on their heads. Of course, those who have been converted later on in life, and who were never baptised as children, can also be baptised, but the normal practice has been the baptism of children. Although to be fair, there are major changes afoot amongst many denominations that have traditionally practised infant baptism. Believers' baptism and baptism by immersion are being offered as an option by more and more churches.

For those brought up in the ecclesiastical "free church" stream, the question is often put: why do other denominations believe and practise baptism of infants when the example of the New Testament was something quite different?

With the exception of the Reformed theological traditions, most other denominations tend to trace their practice of infant baptism back to a theological debate among the early Church fathers (second and third centuries) concerning the effect of "original sin" and the spiritual state of little children. It was their concern that should young children die prematurely before they were baptised, would they be received by God into Paradise?[2] At what point could children of Christian parents be regarded as truly Christian in their own right? Could the parents' faith cover their children from spiritual calamity, and the parents (on their children's behalf) have them baptised in advance?

There is no doubt more that could be said about this to do it justice, but essentially the practice of infant baptism evolved around the third century as a kind of spiritual insurance policy. It was a means of making sure that little children and babies were 'covered' in the event of an untimely death. Later on, when they reached the age of understanding, they could confirm the vows and promises of faith that their parents had made on their behalf at the time of their infant baptism.

God has no grandchildren

At the risk of casting aspersions on the integrity of those Christians and churches that practice baptism of infants, a simple reading of the New Testament makes it difficult to argue that such a practice is truly (or even partially!) defensible.[3] Is it conceivable that the God of love,

---

[2] "The Church has always taught that unbaptized children are excluded from Heaven but has defined nothing as to their positive fate . . . Unbaptized children are buried without liturgical rites in a special part of the cemetery" (Attwater, Catholic Dictionary, p. 255).

[3] "The principle rites in the early Church were Baptism and the Lord's supper. Baptism, it is now generally agreed among scholars, was commonly by immersion. Whether infants were baptized in the Apostolic age, or exactly when the custom arose of administering this rite to them, is a controverted question on which the New Testament writings furnish no direct information" (George P. Fisher, *The Beginnings of Christianity*, p. 565).

mercy, and justice would banish to the fires of Hell little children who had died, simply because they had not been sprinkled with water in a ceremony of baptism? The clear teaching of the New Testament is that salvation is a matter of faith in Jesus Christ, and such faith is a personal decision that each person must come to for themselves. There is nothing parents can do by way of a service or ritual that can substitute for personal choice to follow (or reject) God. Parents are charged with the responsibility of bringing children up in the discipline and instruction of the Lord, and to set a godly example in the home.[4] However, be quite clear on the fact that God has no grandchildren—only children! The faith and devotion of godly parents may give their children a head start toward faith in Christ, but nowhere in the Bible is there a guarantee that the actions of godly parents will secure the salvation of their children.

With Churches of a Reformed theological position, the reasoning for infant baptism is a little different, although the practice is basically the same. It is a Reformed theology position that has argued for a doctrine of infant baptism out of Scripture. In essence, the act of infant baptism is likened to the Old Testament tradition of circumcision. As an act of dedication to Yahweh, and as a sign of God's covenant to be Lord of their child, Jewish parents would present their newborn baby boy to be circumcised. Infant baptism came to be seen as something akin to this, only under the *new covenant*.[5] On the basis of the parent's faith, the newborn baby is presented to the Lord, and baptism is seen as a sign of God's promise to protect and receive the child into his kingdom.

---

[4] Deuteronomy 6:4-7; Psalm 127

[5] In his most renowned work, Institutes of the Christian Religion, John Calvin takes up this issue endeavouring to prove that infant baptism is a divine institution. Calvin declares that "infants cannot be deprived of it [baptism] without open violation of the will of God"(Inst.4, 16, 8). He reasons this primarily through paralleling circumcision and baptism, asserting that Scripture testifies to the fact that baptism is for the Christians what circumcision was previously for the Jews (Inst.4, 16, 11).

Letting the Bible speak for itself, it is difficult to argue for this position without doing all sorts of exegetical gymnastics, such as ignoring the meaning of words and disregarding the earliest traditions and practices of the New Testament Church.

Those churches that practise infant baptism today often lay a great deal of stock on the fact that when Lydia and the Philippian jailer were converted and baptised (Acts 16) their *whole household* or *family* were baptised with them. "Surely," they say, "that must have included little children. Therefore, maybe the New Testament Church did baptise little children after all . . ."

Others argue that such an argument is on very shaky ground when we study the text closely. Leaving aside the gross presumption as to the age of *household* members in Acts 16 (they could well have been a grown-up family) on the occasion of the Philippian jailer's baptism the original Greek text doesn't actually use the word *family* at all. The original word used, as in the case for Lydia's *household,* is the Greek word *oikos*, which by definition was not necessarily limited to family members but included those under one's wider sphere of influence or acquaintance. It could include slaves or servants or close friends as well as close relatives. In other words, those who were with the Philippian jailer or Lydia at the point of their conversion, and who decided along with them to become followers of Jesus, are called their *household*.

Now, it is not the purpose of this book to denigrate those churches that practice infant baptism, except to say that it is hard to deduce its justification from an objective study of New Testament Scripture and early church history. The only pattern we read in the New Testament is the baptism of believers—those who had personally chosen to place their lives under the Lordship of Jesus. Baptism in water was a dramatic declaration of or by those who had had a conversion or spiritual rebirth experience.

When, then, *is* the right time for baptism? The answer is simple:

when a person has come to faith in Jesus. And that is why it is often referred to as "believers' baptism."

That raises another question: How long after one has decided to become a follower of Jesus should water baptism take place? In many churches which practice believers' baptism, often quite some time elapses between a person's conversion experience and the time of their baptism. Several months can go by, in some cases several years. The rationale for this delay has been to give the new convert time to understand more fully the Christian faith. In some cases, it has been viewed as a time when the new convert proves him/herself to be truly changed and transformed, and that his/her profession of faith is not fickle and ephemeral.

Now, one can understand the reason and the rationale for this position, but it is also arguably inconsistent with the New Testament example. The only consistent example we have in the Bible is that baptism followed very closely on the heels of a person's profession of faith in Christ. A person came to faith, and virtually straight away some water was found, and he/she was baptised. That was clearly the example in several places in the Book of Acts. (Ch.2 - Day of Pentecost; Ch.8 - Ethiopian eunuch; Ch.9 - Saul; Ch.10 - Cornelius; Ch.16 - Lydia and the Philippian jailer; etc.)

This New Testament pattern of immediate baptism perhaps raises another important question: How much does a person need to know in order to be ready for baptism? This has no doubt been one of the main reasons for delaying the point of baptism some months after a profession of faith so that a new convert can be trained and educated with the teaching of Scripture. It was also a common practice amongst churches from the second to the fourth century who developed detailed methods of instructing new converts in the ways of Christian faith. However, the answer to the question of requisite accumulation of knowledge, from the New Testament example, must surely be *not much!*

Baptism is not a prize or a diploma which one receives having completed a series of theological studies. It is a dramatic declaration of faith in Christ, and (if the New Testament record is anything to go by) intended to take place as close as practicable to the time of profession of faith. Baptism in water is an act of worship and submission unto the Lord, not a statement of how much a person knows.

Children and baptism

That said, perhaps one exception to the above may be in the case of young children who profess faith in Christ. Here there may be room for charity amidst divergent opinions. While there is no specific biblical text with which to defend such a conviction, many feel uncomfortable with the practice of baptising young children (by immersion), as some churches choose to do. There is no question that young children can commit their lives to Christ in a full and meaningful way, and that spiritual gifts can manifest in children in the exercise of their ministry at a young age. The issue is more one of the significance or "moment" of the believer's baptism declaration, and the potential for it to be cheapened if performed at too early an age. There is also a considerable risk of children doing certain *acts of righteousness* simply because they see their parents doing them, or in order to comply with the wishes of their parents. While there is nothing inherently wrong with this kind of motivation, others suggest how much more significant the baptismal declaration of death and resurrection becomes if performed at an age of understanding and knowledgeable volition. There are many Christians who were baptised as children, who in adult life have a very vague recollection of what should have been a momentous event in their life, and who wish they had waited until an older age.

For the lack of any biblical precedent for delaying baptism of children, some have drawn a parallel with the Jewish age of *bar mitzvah*.

When a young Jewish boy reached the age of twelve, he was permitted to sit with the men in the synagogue and participate in all the acts of worship as an adult. Perhaps a case might be made for making twelve years a minimum age for baptism of Christian children. Consequently, many churches tend to encourage children to wait till their teenage years. On the other hand, some children have been quite insistent that baptism is an act of obedience that Jesus is calling them to make—and something we have little right to deny them.

4. What is the relationship between baptism and belonging to a church family?

In the New Testament, the act of baptism is inextricably related to membership within the Christian Church and is entered into with that understanding. Baptism is not a "stand-alone" sacrament. It is practiced within the fellowship of a group of Christians who are committed to nurturing one another in their faith. Taking the meanings of certain words to an illogical extreme, some might be tempted to see the act of baptism as being performed every time a person is "dunked" in a swimming pool—perhaps even baptising oneself by submerging under water in private. But that is not the act of baptism that the New Testament described.

Baptism in the New Testament Church was performed more as an act of initiation and acceptance. Those who went through the waters of baptism were accepted into the community of those called Christians. They made a public profession or declaration of their faith in Jesus Christ, and this qualified them to partake of the privileges and responsibilities of church life. Baptism was an act of submission and obedience toward Jesus, but also a declaration in front of witnesses. In that sense, a baptism in private or with no one to witness it is a contradiction in terms.

We considered earlier the words of Paul to the Church in Corinth on baptism and the body of Christ; note again the relationship between the two that Paul alludes to:

> [12] *Just as a body, though one, has many parts, but all its many parts form one body, so it is with Christ.* [13] *For we were all baptized by one Spirit so as to form one body—whether Jews or Gentiles, slave or free—and we were all given the one Spirit to drink.*
>
> 1 Corinthians 12:12,13

Through baptism, we are united or enmeshed within the many-faceted body of Christ. Those who are baptised are recognised as belonging to the family of God, having testified to their own personal faith in Jesus Christ, and are not merely the sons and daughters of Christians, or those living within a defined parochial district. Baptism in water has been viewed as a sign or testimony of that regeneration, which again is why it is often referred to as *believers' baptism.*

For this reason, historically there is a very strong link between baptism and formal church membership. From earliest years, the vast majority of people who are baptised in water also become official church members. Conversely, in some churches, it is not possible to become a formal member without having first been baptised. This is not to be exclusionary, as much as to establish a baseline for interpreting the meaning of *"baptised by one Spirit into one body."*

There are obvious difficulties in holding too stringently to this view, as some people have refrained from being baptised in water yet are very evidently part of the Kingdom of God. Some ask, with good reason, whether it is right that such people should be refused the opportunity to become church members irrespective of baptism. If they are accepted by God into his family, why shouldn't they be allowed to number themselves amongst their local church family—as full members? That is a fair question, but so also is the question of why they choose to disregard the clear instruction of Scripture on the matter of baptism in the first place!

The matter of formal church membership is something some in the contemporary church have difficulty with. *"If I am a part of the worldwide family of God why do I need to join a local Church?"* There certainly isn't a proof text to justify membership rolls, but that doesn't necessarily make it wrong either. The New Testament Church certainly did have some means of determining who was, and who was not, a part of their community. They also repeatedly counted, and recorded, the number of Christians in their pastoral care. The idea of church membership, it is argued, is simply a contemporary expression of the New Testament principle of belonging to, and commitment toward, a local body of believers. In the same way that a public marriage service formalises the commitments of love and faithfulness that an engaged couple makes several times to each other in private, so the formal act of becoming a church member is a significant public commitment of an individual to his/her church and the church to an individual. There are many Christians today who instead choose to follow the worldly pattern and live in a *de facto* relationship with their church!

Throwing the baby out with the bathwater

Of course, the whole concept of church is undergoing a metamorphosis in our day and age. Some are expressing disillusionment with the idea of belonging to a local church community. Numbers of people claim to be Christians but are simply opting out of any involvement in a local fellowship, or at best attend only spasmodically. They like Jesus . . . but they're not sure they like his wife! On the one hand, there is room for sympathy for such people, as in many cases contemporary church life may bear little resemblance to the movement Jesus started two thousand years ago. On the other hand, however, some people are *"throwing out the baby with the bath water."* The contemporary Church may not always be what God wants it to be, but it is still the body of Christ. Furthermore, to be Christian means by definition to be "in fellowship" with other believers. Disillusionment or disenchantment with churches, even deep hurt from painful abuse, is never a justification for disregarding biblical teaching on fellowship and belonging to a local expression of the body of Christ.

All of this has major ramifications for determining the place and method of baptising new converts. Traditionally (at least for the past few hundred years or more) it has tended to take place in a church worship service. This has given the receiving congregation the opportunity to witness the testimony of faith, and to accept the new believer into the fellowship of the Church. But is it the only situation where baptism could/should take place? An alternative has been for baptisms to occur in a more informal setting, such as the local beach or river, or in a swimming pool. And when we consider the baptisms of new converts that are recorded in the Book of Acts, there is some justification as none of these were in what we might describe today as a worship service. There are great advantages in testifying to one's faith in front of a congregation in a church service, but so also in an informal setting in the context of a small group or in front of an extended family.

Traditionally, baptism has been a sacrament of the Church administered by ordained clergy, but this actually has very little biblical warrant. It could be argued that Jesus himself was baptised by an uneducated wilderness renegade, and many of the "baptisers" in the book of Acts appear to be ordinary Christians without any special ecclesiastical credentials. In fact, for a model of the relationship between church leadership and baptism, we can look at the Apostle Paul.

He seemed to be quite deliberate in not performing the baptisms of many converts. He didn't want people forming an emotional attachment to him as the one by whom they were baptised, so he got other people in the "body" to do it instead.[6] If the New Testament is our guide it is not the exclusive prerogative of pastors to perform the act of baptism in a church community. Better to involve people who have played a significant part in the conversion process of the new convert —perhaps a parent or close friend or small group leader.

But it is still important that water baptism be a sacrament owned by the local church and performed under the pastoral oversight of a church's leadership. At times we may want to shift the location and timing outside of church buildings. However, the theological principle of baptism as an initiation into the Body of Christ implies that it be conducted under the delegated oversight of the leaders of the church. They may wish to delegate the process to a small group (or other) leader, but it is not something that should be done without their knowledge or blessing.

5. What about those who have been Christians for many years, but have never been baptised?

We can no doubt all call to mind some very godly people, with wonderful character and ministries, who have never been through the waters of believers' baptism. If the Bible presents it so clearly, and yet these people are still so effective in their service for God, is baptism really that important? Or to put it another way, is it really necessary that mature Christians, who were not baptised at the time of their conversion,

---

[6] 1 Corinthians 1:14-16

go through the motions of believers' baptism some years later?

Obviously, answers to these kinds of questions are contentious. There are some who advocate that they must, and there are others who say that it is superfluous. For many, the act of *confirmation* (usually in teenage years) was a significant equivalent to baptism in water. There they publicly confessed their faith in Jesus and confirmed the promises that their parents spoke over them when they were baptised as a baby.

If you're in that position reading this book, rest assured that its purpose is not to put you under pressure, except to suggest that it might be an issue for which you discover the mind of the Lord. Being baptised is a matter of obedience to Christ's command, and must be done unto the Lord, not unto the church. The motive is all important—do it for His sake, not for anyone else's.

This book obviously takes the position that baptism is relevant for all Christians, regardless of how long after their conversion-experience it occurs. The biblical pattern was straight away, but in situations where that did not (or could not) occur, there is a place for the mature Christian going back to that point where they missed out and, in the words of Jesus, *"fulfilling all righteousness"*. Many, who have belonged to Churches (traditions) where believers' baptism was not taught or practised, when exposed to biblical exposition on baptism have felt a definite conviction from the Lord that they too should be baptised. Done as an act of obedience to Jesus, it has unlocked all manner of blessing and renewal in their Christian walk.

There are some who object to this as an unnecessary re-baptising of people who have already been baptised. In actual fact, there might be a biblical precedent for the re-baptising of those who were "done" (as it were) as infants. In Acts 19 we read the story of Paul arriving at Ephesus and finding a small group of believers:

> [1] *...There he found some disciples* [2] *and asked them, "Did you receive the Holy Spirit when you believed?"*

> *They answered, "No, we have not even heard that there is a Holy Spirit."*
> *³ So Paul asked, "Then what baptism did you receive?"*
> *"John's baptism," they replied.*
> *⁴ Paul said, "John's baptism was a baptism of repentance. He told the people to believe in the one coming after him, that is, in Jesus." ⁵ On hearing this, they were baptized into the name of the Lord Jesus. ⁶ When Paul placed his hands on them, the Holy Spirit came on them, and they spoke in tongues and prophesied. ⁷ There were about twelve men in all.*
>
> *Acts 19:1-7*

Here was a group of people who had been earnestly seeking God and had had a form of baptism at the hands of John the Baptist. But when they accepted Jesus, Paul didn't recognise their former baptism as the type of baptism practised in the emerging Christian community. Instead, he re-baptised them in the mode and the name of Jesus. In a similar vein, it has been suggested, there is a valid argument for re-baptising those who were earlier baptised as infants, on the grounds that infant baptism is a form of baptism that cannot be reconciled with New Testament theology or practice. Therefore, believers' baptism is not in actual fact a second baptism, but a first.

There are, of course, all sorts of other reasons why people who have been Christians for many years choose not to be baptised. For some, it may simply be a matter of pride. The issue really is a personal one between an individual and the Lord, and we can have every confidence in God's ability to bring about the right conviction for the right action at the right time.

If you are a follower of Jesus and have not yet gone through the waters of baptism, here is a challenge for you to consider doing so in the near future. What is it that stops you? There will be those who will encourage you to see it as unimportant or even unnecessary. If you were to pray and ask God his opinion, what do you think his answer might be? The choice is yours to make, and so are the consequences. Perhaps the question to consider is: Are we brave enough to challenge a direct command of Jesus!

> *. . . Go into all the world and preach the good news to all creation. ¹⁶ Whoever believes and is baptized will be saved, but whoever does not believe will be condemned . . .*
>
> *Mark 16:15,16*

Part Two

Two

The Person and Work of the Holy Spirit

It was Jesus who said that when an old wineskin is filled with new wine, it leaks.[7] The chemical properties and fermentation of the new wine cause the old wineskins to crack and split open as they become hard and inflexible and cannot tolerate the vitality of the new wine. God is perpetually doing a new thing among his people,[8] and sometimes the old containers or vessels that carried what he did yesterday are not suitable for what he wants to do tomorrow. It is a constant challenge for the church to keep up with what God is doing; not lagging behind or longing

---

[7] Cf. Matthew 9:17; Mark 2:22; Luke 5:37
[8] Isaiah 43:19

for another spin on the merry-go-round of yesteryear.

The era of the Christian Church that we live in today is particularly exciting. It is characterised by a number of new movements and one of those is the widespread renewal of the ministries and spiritual gifts that we read about in the New Testament. Christians from all walks of life and church traditions have experienced a fresh touch of the Holy Spirit, and it has radically changed their lives. The so-called *charismatic renewal* has been truly world-wide and trans-denominational over the past several decades. God has poured new wine into his Church, and those who have been wise enough to catch it with new wineskins have seen the nature and vitality of their churches transformed. Sadly, some churches have missed out on this contemporary outpouring of God's Spirit because of intransigent attitudes and closed theological minds. In these situations, the new wine has begun to leak out, and churches that refused to receive it are today characterised by declining patronage.

Central to this era of spiritual renewal has been a renewed focus on the person and ministry of the Holy Spirit, and in particular, a desire to understand and experience what it means to be empowered by him in order to serve God. For many Christians, there has been an unspoken credibility gap between the historical record of the early Church and our experience today. The Book of Acts, for instance, describes a Christian Church that was passionate for God, and amongst whom manifestations of God's power were commonplace and far from unusual. Yet in so many churches today something similar does not appear to be happening. Why is that the case? Why are we not experiencing the same endowment of Holy Spirit power and manifestation in our Christian experience as those first Christians did? Why are we not seeing numbers of people coming to faith in Christ as the early Church appeared to experience?

A big part of the answer to these questions has to do with our understanding of the ministry of the Holy Spirit. For too long there has been a lack of clear teaching on who he is, how he indwells Christians and empowers them to minister in the name of Jesus. The objective of this book is to offer simple biblical exposition for ordinary Christians, in our day and age, as to how they can also experience the outpouring of Holy Spirit power as did those first believers.

Understanding the context is crucial

In order to do that we need to go back to the original context in which the Christian Church first encountered the Holy Spirit. This context was the assignment that Jesus gave his first band of disciples. Prior to his ascension into heaven (after his resurrection), Jesus left his followers an enormous task. They were to carry on his ministry and preach the good news about God's love for mankind to the entire world, making disciples of every nation. It was an enormous assignment and continues to this day as the commission passes from one generation of the church to the next. But before he left them Jesus gave them a crucial piece of advice. He told them that before they did anything they were to sit tight and wait for the Holy Spirit to come upon them. When that had happened, they would have the power they needed to fulfil their task:

> [4] . . . "Do not leave Jerusalem, but wait for the gift my Father promised, which you have heard me speak about. [5] For John baptized with water, but in a few days you will be baptized with the Holy Spirit . . ."
> [8] ". . .you will receive power when the Holy Spirit comes on you; and you will be my witnesses in Jerusalem, and in all Judea and Samaria, and to the ends of the earth."
> Acts 1:4-5,8

In order to fulfil their assignment of world evangelisation they needed an encounter with the Spirit of God. Before they could be witnesses to Jesus in their community, and out to the ends of the earth, they needed to experience an infusion of God's power as the Holy Spirit came upon them. The second chapter of the Book of Acts records how that dramatic encounter began, and the rest of Acts tells the story of what happened as a result. We will look at that in more detail later on.

The advice Jesus gave those first believers still stands for you and me today. We do not need to go back to Jerusalem in order to get it, but the task of reaching our world with the good news of Jesus Christ is still our responsibility. Therefore, if the task is still current, so also must be the enabling power of God so that we can fulfil it. If we are to see our community and world transformed by the saving power of Jesus Christ, we desperately need an encounter with the Holy Spirit like those first-generation believers experienced.

The two most consistent New Testament phrases that describe that encounter are being *baptised in the Holy Spirit* or being *filled with the Holy Spirit*. As noted, one of the sad features of church life in many places has been the neglect of teaching on the ministry of the Holy Spirit. Many believers have never known of their need, let alone their invitation, to be filled with the Spirit, which has been described as like having mains-electricity connected to your house, but never having thrown the switch to turn it on!

Another sad reality has been controversy and division that teaching on the ministry of the Holy Spirit has caused in churches. When you mention the phrase *baptism in the Holy Spirit* in certain churches people move forward an inch or two on their seats. "How is this subject going to be dealt with? Am I going to be able to stay in this church after hearing what the preacher has to say?" Perhaps it's worth noting an apparent strategy of the evil one: the greater the truth the more the devil will seek to cause controversy and division surrounding it. And that surely has been the case when it comes to the empowering ministry of the Spirit of God. If the reason for being filled with the Spirit is so we can fulfil our assignment of making disciples of every nation, it stands to reason that the devil will do all he can to surround it with conflict.

Baptism or fullness in the Holy Spirit is part of the whole counsel of God's Word, and therefore we need to study it and be open to appropriate it. Dr. Billy Graham summed it up well many years ago when he made the following comment:

> *"The time has come to give the Holy Spirit his rightful place. We need to learn what it means to be baptised with the Holy Spirit, we need to know what Paul means when he says: 'Be filled with the Holy Spirit'. Give it any terminology you like, we need to accept it, to get something, for we do not have the same dynamic that the early Church had."* [9]

As we delve into this subject, we must keep our minds as open as possible to receiving new truth from the Scriptures. Some reading this book will come from church backgrounds where such teaching is regarded as dubious and divisive; while others come from churches where they seem to teach nothing else but baptism in the Holy Spirit! Somewhere in between is the right balance. It also needs to be noted that a subject like this is extremely broad. Vast numbers of books have been written on the person and ministry of the Holy Spirit, and it is not the intention of this work to repeat all that they have to say. Where we need to begin, however, is right back at the basics—assuming we know nothing about the Holy Spirit, and then building from there.

There are two foundational questions that this chapter poses; the significance of which will be built on in the remaining chapters:

1. What exactly do we mean by the term Holy Spirit?
2. What does the Holy Spirit actually do?

In Christian circles we bandy around a lot of in-house jargon; words and phrases that have meaning and content for the initiated, but

---

[9] David Watson, *"One in the Spirit"*, (Hodder & Stoughton, 1973), p.20.

for those new to the faith they are somewhat confusing. That is true when Christians talk about the Holy Spirit, so let's go right back to the basics and ask the kind of questions some might feel too embarrassed to ask.

1. What do we mean by the term Holy Spirit?

Firstly, we are talking about God. The Holy Spirit is the Spirit of God—a member of what we call the Trinity. *He* is one of the three distinct ways that God reveals or manifests himself in our world. We refer to God (who is one) as *Father*, *Son* and *Holy Spirit*.

Once again, the doctrine of the Trinity is an extremely large subject that we're not going to deal adequately with here. Suffice it to say, we ought not to neglect this member of the Godhead in our speech and prayers and our understanding of God's nature. Although we may not always understand the mysterious relationship between each member of the Trinity, we recognise that each has a particular place and function.

It has been suggested that the Holy Spirit has sometimes been the displaced person of the Trinity; forgotten or left out of our speech and thinking. For instance, the make-up of the Trinity for the Catholic Church, it has rather cynically been described, is *Father*, *Son* and *Holy Virgin*. Similarly, for some overly zealous Protestants as *God the Father*, *God the Son* and *God his Holy Word*. We need to affirm and address the Holy Spirit as being as much a part of the Godhead as the Father and the Son.

Secondly, when we talk about the Holy Spirit we are talking about a person. Sometimes people wrongly refer to the Holy Spirit by impersonal and inanimate terms such as "it" or "power" or "force". The Holy Spirit is not an impersonal inanimate *thing*; *he* is a person of the

Godhead, and we must refer to him in the same way as we do to the Father and the Son with pronouns of *person*-ality. We sometimes use word pictures or metaphors of inanimate things to describe the activity and effect of the Holy Spirit, and this no doubt gives rise to some confusion. There are at least five such metaphors found in the Bible: *fire, wind, oil, water* and *love*. But these are simply word pictures to describe the impact of the person of the Holy Spirit on people or the world around us.

The Bible is quite clear on the fact that the Holy Spirit has all the characteristics of personality and personhood. Here are four examples:

(i) *Thought:* Romans 8:37 — Paul speaks of the *mind* of the Spirit.
(ii) *Speech:* Acts 8:29 — The Spirit *said* to Philip 'Go up and join this chariot . . .'
Acts 13:2 — The Holy Spirit *said*, 'Set apart to me Paul and Barnabas' . . .
(iii) *Action:* Romans 8:14 — Paul says that those who are sons of God are *led* by the Spirit . . .
1 Corinthians 12:11 — Speaks of the Spirit apportioning gifts to each one as he *wills* . . .
(iv) *Feelings:* Romans 15:30 — Paul speaks of the *love* of the Spirit . . .
Ephesians 4:30 — We can *grieve* the Spirit . . .
1 Thessalonians 5:19 — We can *quench* the Spirit . . ."

All of these are characteristics of personhood. A power or force does not think or speak. It may act, but you cannot hurt its feelings. However, the Spirit of God does all of these things. The renowned preacher R.A. Torrey put it well when he said:

"If you think of him only as an influence you will be anxious

that you may have more of `it'. But if you think of him as a person, you will desire that he may have more of you!" [10]

Some of the talk about baptism in the Holy Spirit in recent years may have given a wrong impression in this regard. Some preachers have implied that it is more of something we get from God, like a commodity or a product. While it is true that we do want more of the Spirit and more of his power, maybe a better emphasis would be to think in terms of how he can have more of us.

2. What does the Holy Spirit actually do?

We've established a little of whom *he* is and what *he* is like, but what is the Holy Spirit's actual function? We often talk in terms of the ministry of the Holy Spirit. What does that really mean?

According to the Scriptures, there is a long list of functions or ministries that the Holy Spirit performs. Over the years vast volumes have been written describing and outlining all that he does. What follows is far from a comprehensive list of the Holy Spirit's ministries; instead, we focus on two brief statements of Jesus, as recorded by the Apostle John. In John 14 Jesus gave his disciples these instructions concerning the function of the Holy Spirit, whom the Father was to give them after his ascension:

> [15] "If you love me, keep my commands. [16] And I will ask the Father, and he will give you another advocate to help you and be with you forever— [17] the Spirit of truth. The world cannot accept him, because it neither sees him nor knows him. But you know him, for he lives with you and will be in you.
>
> John 14:15-17

Then in John 16, Jesus spoke this way about the coming Holy

---

[10] David Watson, *"One in the Spirit"*, (Hodder & Stoughton, 1973), p.25.

Spirit:

> ⁷ *But very truly I tell you, it is for your good that I am going away. Unless I go away, the Advocate will not come to you; but if I go, I will send him to you. ⁸ When he comes, he will prove the world to be in the wrong about sin and righteousness and judgment . . .*
> *John 16:7-8*

There are four important functions of the Holy Spirit mentioned in these verses that need to be underscored:

Counsellor

The original Greek word translated here as counsellor is *parakletos*, which is variously translated as *comforter, divine helper, advocate, lawyer, intercessor, comforter,* or *strengthener*. Literally, it meant "a calling to one's side."[11] It described someone who comes to the assistance of another and helps or assists him in doing what he is doing. Jesus said that this is the ministry of the Holy Spirit: he is one who comes alongside us and helps us in our responsibilities as disciples of Jesus.

Whatever Jesus asks of us as his followers, we are never left to do it on our own. When he gives us a function or a ministry or a prompting to say or do something, we always have the *paraklete* alongside to help us do it. That is an incredibly comforting thought - we are never on our own. To put it another way, the Holy Spirit is a bit like our personal coach. He is our trainer or mentor, constantly there with us and giving us instructions on how to play the game and overcome our opponent. We are never alone or defenceless in our spiritual battles because the Holy Spirit is constantly with us, helping us fulfil whatever God asks of us.

---

[11] W.E. Vine, *"An Expository Dictionary of New Testament Words,"* (Riverside Book and Bible House, Iowa, 1939), p.200

Spirit of Truth

Jesus said that the Holy Spirit is the Spirit of *Truth* who will guide us into all truth. One of the important functions of the Holy Spirit is to help us understand or discern right from wrong. He gives us the ability to differentiate between what is true and what is false. We can tell the difference between behaviour that is godly and that which is ungodly. When we are faced with many choices and crossroads, it is a function of the Holy Spirit to guide us into the right choices when we turn to him for counsel.

In the world we live in today there are many different sets of values and philosophies that are presented as normal and natural. We live in an age of moral relativism: How is a person able to tell which is the right way to turn? How are we to make the right choices in life? The good news is that God has not left us alone. He has given us his Spirit who guides us into all truth. When we read the Scriptures, it is a function of the Holy Spirit to open our eyes to truths that we have never understood before. Perhaps you have had the experience of reading a passage of Scripture, and something leaps out at you from the printed page. It seems as if what was written there several thousand years ago is just for you! That is the work of the Spirit of Truth.

In our dealings with people, it is the function of the Holy Spirit to whisper words of caution (or encouragement) when we are presented with options of behaviour. The Spirit of truth speaks directly into our conscience. He addresses *our* spirit. Sometimes we do not really know why we think a particular choice or direction is wrong, but something deep down inside us is warning us. That is the Spirit of Truth at work in us as followers of Jesus; a ministry of the Holy Spirit.

Convicts of sin

Jesus said that it is the work of the Holy Spirit in us that convicts us of our wrongdoing and our need of God's forgiveness.[12] The Holy Spirit opens our eyes or illuminates our conscience so that we cannot avoid recognising our own wrongdoing.

Becoming a follower of Jesus and having our sins forgiven and cleansed is only partly our doing. Most of the work is actually done by God the Holy Spirit. If it was left up to us, we probably wouldn't have bothered about having our relationship with God straightened out. We might not have noticed how our life was an insult to him. But the work of the Holy Spirit was to convince us of our need to be in a right relationship with God. He worked on our conscience and on our will, making us dissatisfied with our lives and aware of our disobedience and rebellion against him.

In our efforts in evangelism, it is always important to remember that we cannot convince anybody to become a Christian, no matter how clever our argument or eloquent our presentation. That act of opening eyes to the truth and convincing people of their need for God is the work of the Holy Spirit. Better that we talk in terms of our cooperating with the Holy Spirit in the work of evangelising our community. He is the one who really does the work. At best we can cooperate; most often our feeble efforts just get in the way!

Indwells us

Perhaps this is the most significant aspect of his ministry to us. The Holy Spirit dwells or lives inside the true believer. God is not distant and far off from us. If Jesus is Lord of our life, the Holy Spirit has been deposited in us. The Apostle Paul put it this way in his writings to the Christians in Corinth:

> [16] *Don't you know that you yourselves are God's temple and that God's Spirit dwells in your midst?*

---

[12] John 8:46; 1 Thessalonian 1:5

> *1 Corinthians 3:16*

> *²¹ . . . He anointed us, ²² set his seal of ownership on us, and put his Spirit in our hearts as a deposit, guaranteeing what is to come.*
> *2 Corinthians 1:21-22*

> *⁵ Now the one who has fashioned us for this very purpose is God, who has given us the Spirit as a deposit, guaranteeing what is to come.*
> *2 Corinthians 5:5*

That, of course, is a two-edged sword. On the one hand, it is great having God constantly with us for advice and counsel. But on the other hand, it means that we take God with us wherever we go. He sees what our eyes rest on, and he hears what comes out of our mouth. He is constantly with us in all we do. Did he want to go into all the places and situations we took him into this past week?

On the positive side of the ledger, having the indwelling presence of the Holy Spirit in our life means that all the potential power of God is resident within us. All that Jesus did in the power of the Holy Spirit two-thousand years ago is the potential for us also. The same Spirit of Jesus is given to us who are his followers. That certainly was how Jesus saw it:

> *Very truly I tell you, all who have faith in me will do the works I have been doing, and they will do even greater things than these, because I am going to the Father.*
> *John 14:12*

Immediately following that statement Jesus went on to talk about the coming of the Holy Spirit in the passage we read earlier.

It's worth stopping to ask ourselves: have we really taken note of what Jesus was saying here? Have we fully grasped hold of the fact that the very same capacity as Jesus had for mercy and love, and the very same potential for power and working miracles, is the birthright of every person who is born again of the Spirit of God? The same Holy Spirit that indwelt our Lord Jesus resides in each of us.

To put it more graphically, the mains electricity has been connected. The crucial question is this: Have we thrown the switch and turned it on?

Three

Baptism in the Holy Spirit

Immediately prior to Jesus' Ascension into heaven, he gave his disciples a commission: they (and those who came after them) were to carry on the work that he had begun. The Apostle John records it with these words:

> [21] *... As the Father sent me, I am sending you ...*
> *John 20:21*

The mission that the Father gave to Jesus, he in turn, passed on to his disciples. They (we!) were to carry on the work that Jesus had been doing, making disciples of all nations, preaching the gospel to the whole of creation. But when Jesus gave his disciples this enormous assignment, he did not merely give them a job description, and say, "Go to it!" He also gave them the tools of the trade. He gave them the means or the power they would need to carry on his work and fulfil their assignment.

Immediately following the statement, "As the Father sent me, I am sending you", John records that Jesus breathed on them, and said, "Receive the Holy Spirit". In other words: "To be able to fulfil this assignment that I am giving you, you need to have the resources and power that I have been operating under."

If we go to Luke's version of what happened immediately prior to Jesus' ascension into heaven, we get a similar picture. In Acts 1 Luke records Jesus' counsel to his disciples to wait in Jerusalem until the Holy Spirit had come upon them. When that had happened, they would have the power and resources to carry out the task Jesus was giving them.

We cannot fulfil God's expectations of us as Christians without the dynamic activity of the Holy Spirit, working in us and on us. In order to witness effectively for God, in order to resist the temptations and snares of the devil, in order to be able to love others the way God does, in order to pray for the sick and confront demonic activity, we need an empowering encounter with the Holy Spirit. Jesus told his disciples that before they could do any of these things they had to sit tight and wait for the Holy Spirit to come upon them. So that is what they did until it happened.

The second chapter of the Book of Acts describes how those first believers experienced the coming of the Holy Spirit upon them:

> [1] *When the day of Pentecost came, they were all together in one place.* [2] *Suddenly a sound like the blowing of a violent wind came from heaven and filled the whole house where they were sitting.* [3] *They saw what seemed to be tongues of fire that separated and came to rest on each of them.* [4] *All of them were filled with the Holy Spirit and began to speak in other tongues as the Spirit enabled them.*

⁵ Now there were staying in Jerusalem God-fearing Jews from every nation under heaven. ⁶ When they heard this sound, a crowd came together in bewilderment, because each one heard their own language being spoken. ⁷ Utterly amazed, they asked: "Aren't all these who are speaking Galileans? ⁸ Then how is it that each of us hears them in our native language? ⁹ Parthians, Medes and Elamites; residents of Mesopotamia, Judea and Cappadocia, Pontus and Asia, [b] ¹⁰ Phrygia and Pamphylia, Egypt and the parts of Libya near Cyrene; visitors from Rome ¹¹ (both Jews and converts to Judaism); Cretans and Arabs—we hear them declaring the wonders of God in our own tongues!" ¹² Amazed and perplexed, they asked one another, "What does this mean?"

¹³ Some, however, made fun of them and said, "They have had too much wine."

¹⁴ Then Peter stood up with the Eleven, raised his voice and addressed the crowd: "Fellow Jews and all of you who live in Jerusalem, let me explain this to you; listen carefully to what I say. ¹⁵ These people are not drunk, as you suppose. It's only nine in the morning! ¹⁶ No, this is what was spoken by the prophet Joel: ¹⁷ " 'In the last days, God says, I will pour out my Spirit on all people. Your sons and daughters will prophesy, your young men will see visions, your old men will dream dreams. ¹⁸ Even on my servants, both men and women, I will pour out my Spirit in those days, and they will prophesy. ¹⁹ I will show wonders in the heaven above and signs on the earth below, blood and fire and billows of smoke. ²⁰ The sun will be turned to darkness and the moon to blood before the coming of the great and glorious day of the Lord. And everyone who calls on the name of the Lord will be saved.'

Acts 2:1-21

Peter then gave a spontaneous and powerful gospel apologetic on the life of Jesus, showing how he fulfilled so much ancient prophecy concerning the predicted Messiah. His message was particularly anointed, and a vast crowd came under deep conviction:

> [37] *When the people heard this, they were cut to the heart and said to Peter and the other apostles, "Brothers, what shall we do?"*
> [38] *Peter replied, "Repent and be baptized, every one of you, in the name of Jesus Christ for the forgiveness of your sins. And you will receive the gift of the Holy Spirit.* [39] *The promise is for you and your children and for all who are far off—for all whom the Lord our God will call."*
> [40] *With many other words, he warned them; and he pleaded with them, "Save yourselves from this corrupt generation."* [41] *Those who accepted his message were baptized, and about three thousand were added to their number that day.*
>
> Acts 2:37-41

The rest of the Book of Acts tells the story of what happened as a result of that dramatic day. Something in the lives of those initial believers changed on the Day of Pentecost. A radical transformation took place. People who were fairly sheepish followers of Jesus all of a sudden became fearless proclaimers of the Gospel. They laid their hands upon sick people, and they got well; they preached powerfully in front of thousands of people, even in the face of fierce opposition and persecution; they had a boldness and an energy that just simply was not there before.

Quite obviously the factor that changed them was a personal experience of the Holy Spirit on the Day of Pentecost. Before that encounter, they were people who knew the Lord and his teaching and commission, but for all intents and purposes were powerless to do anything with it. After Pentecost, they had a power and a passion in their belly that literally turned the city of Jerusalem upside down.

History or current affairs?

The account in Acts 2 poses an important question: *How should we interpret the events of the Day of Pentecost?* Was it a unique event in history—the birth of the Christian Church? Was it an experience of the Holy Spirit that happened once—something unique, not to be repeated? Or was it an initiatory event that illustrates something of what should be the experience of all believers from that day onwards? In other words, when we read the second chapter of Acts are we merely reading historical narrative, or are we reading about an empowering encounter that is the birthright of every believer?

The answer, many contend, is both! The events of the Day of Pentecost *are* unique and special. It was the birthing of the Christian Church, and therefore needs to be viewed as a day special in history. We cannot expect to be able to recapture the Pentecost experience in our setting. However, the effect of the coming of the Holy Spirit on the lives of those first believers is a clear illustration of what can be our experience also.

That is certainly how the Apostle Peter saw it. After he had preached his spontaneous evangelistic message to the crowd that had gathered to see the commotion, hundreds of people responded, asking him what they should do to be right with God. Note again his prediction of what they would experience, as those touched on the Day of Pentecost had been, if they truly repented:

> [38] "... and you will receive the gift of the Holy Spirit. [39] The promise is for you and your children and for all who are far off—for all whom the Lord our God will call."
>
> *Acts 2:38, 39*

The exact nature of the encounter might differ, but the fact or need of a personal, dynamic experience of the Holy Spirit is something Peter saw as being for all Christians. As mentioned in the previous chapter, the most consistent phrase in the New Testament that describes that empowering encounter is the phrase *baptised in the Holy Spirit* or *being filled with the Holy Spirit*. But what exactly does that mean, and how do we go about appropriating it?

1. Confusion over terminology

The phrase *baptised in/with the Holy Spirit* is found six times in the New Testament; once in each of the four Gospels and twice in the book of Acts. In each instance in the Gospels it is John the Baptist speaking prophetically of what Jesus will do:

> *I baptise you with water for repentance. But after me comes one who is more powerful than I, whose sandals I am not worthy to carry. He will baptise you with the Holy Spirit and fire.*
>
> Matthew 3:11[13]

In Acts, the first mention is Acts 1:4, 5:

> *⁴ On one occasion, while he was eating with them, he gave them this command: "Do not leave Jerusalem, but wait for the gift my Father promised, which you have heard me speak about. ⁵ For John baptized with water, but in a few days you will be baptized with the Holy Spirit."*

The second reference to *baptism in the Holy Spirit* in Acts is found in Acts 11:16 where Peter recalls what Jesus said in Acts 1.

The first point to be established, then, is that the phrase *baptism in the Holy Spirit* is a biblical phrase and describes a valid Christian experience. Some church leaders, resistant to the new wine God is pouring into his church, have rather foolishly asserted that the

---

[13] Cf: Mark 1:8, Luke 3:16, John 1:33

phrase (let alone the experience) is not biblical. It is, and therefore we need to wrestle with what it means.

Definition

As to the definition of words, we noted in Chapter One that the word baptise comes from the Greek word *baptizo*, meaning literally to *immerse* or *dip*. To be baptised in the Holy Spirit therefore means literally to be dipped or immersed in the person and nature of the Holy Spirit; being absolutely saturated with him.

What Jesus said to the disciples in Acts 1 about waiting in Jerusalem until they were baptised with the Holy Spirit, obviously found fulfilment on the Day of Pentecost. On that day those initial believers (numbering around 120) were baptised with the Holy Spirit. It was the first fulfilment of what John the Baptist, and Jesus, had predicted would happen. As we've already noted, it was also regarded by those first recipients of the Holy Spirit as something that *"all whom the Lord our God would call"* would experience also. That would seem to include you and me! We too are meant to experience the gift of the Spirit and what it means to be immersed in him.

When we read on in the Book of Acts there are at least six occasions where the Holy Spirit manifested himself in an initiation-type experience to new believers. These are situations where new Christians were baptised with the Holy Spirit. It's interesting to note the different terminology that is used to describe these encounters. The experience is given a variety of names, but seems to stand for the same thing:

> Acts 2:4 (Day of Pentecost) *". . . all of them were **filled** with the Holy Spirit . . ."*
> Acts 2:38 (Peter's Pentecost sermon) *". . . you will **receive** the gift of the Holy Spirit . . ."*

> Acts 8:15 (Peter ministering to some Samaritans) *". . .prayed that they might **receive** the Holy Spirit . . ."*
> Acts 9:17 (Paul's conversion) *". . . be **filled** with the Holy Spirit . . ."*
> Acts 10:44-48 (Peter preaching to Cornelius) *". . . the Holy Spirit **came upon** them . . ."*
> *". . . the Holy Spirit had been **poured out** on them . . ."*
> Acts 19:1-7 (Paul preaching to some Ephesians) *". . . the Holy Spirit **came on** them . . ."*

The point to note is that actual terminology used to describe the experience of being baptised with the Holy Spirit is varied and largely immaterial. There are a variety of phrases in the New Testament record that seem to describe the same thing. Taking some of our heroes in the Christian faith in recent centuries, men of God over the years have referred to their own experience using different terminology. For instance, men like D.L. Moody, R.A. Torrey, William Booth, Andrew Murray, George Whitefield, and Charles Finney apparently preferred the phrase *baptism in the Holy Spirit* to describe their experience. Others like Campbell Morgan and Charles Spurgeon preferred the phrase *being filled with Holy Spirit*. In other words, the handle we give it does not matter very much. The important point is: Can we say that we have experienced it for ourselves? Have we been baptised or filled or immersed or anointed or released or empowered by the Holy Spirit in order to fulfil our mission from God? If the answer to that question is "no" (or "not sure"), then the next question is: *Are we prepared to be?*

2. What happens when we're filled with the Holy Spirit?

The noted British Bible teacher, David Pawson, once gave an interesting answer when someone asked him the question: "What happens to you when you get baptised in the Spirit?" His response: *"Trouble!"* Sad to say, more than a few churches have split in half over someone claiming an experience like that of the Day of Pentecost.

The real answer to that question, however, is *power!* That was clearly Jesus' intention when he told the disciples to wait in Jerusalem:

> *8 . . . you will receive power when the Holy Spirit comes on you; and you will be my witnesses in Jerusalem, and in all Judea and Samaria, and to the ends of the earth."*
>
> Acts 1:8

Being filled or baptised in the Holy Spirit is synonymous with being endued with the power of God. The *paraklete* comes alongside us and empowers or enables us to fulfil what God asks of us. If we want to be a people used effectively for God, and in the work of his Kingdom, then the place to start is being endued with his power.

Note the following examples from the Book of Acts of how being filled with the Spirit resulted in power-filled ministry:
- In Acts 1:8 Jesus specifically talks about power to *witness* or testify about one's faith experience. Being baptised in the Spirit gives us power to be a better witness for Jesus.
- In Acts 2:4, on the Day of Pentecost, being filled with the Spirit results in people having a supernatural ability to speak a foreign language. They speak the message of the gospel in *tongues* they have never learned.
- In Acts 2:14-41 Peter is emboldened to get up and *preach* a spontaneous evangelistic message that resulted in 3000 people coming to know the Lord.
- In Acts 3:1-10 Peter and John perform an outstanding *healing miracle* on a lame beggar.

- In Acts 4:8-20 Peter and John have power and courage from the Holy Spirit to fearlessly *continue proclaiming the good news in the face of persecution* and physical beatings.
- In Acts 5:1-11 Peter is given special insight and *knowledge* that a couple by name of Ananias and Sapphira are lying—and when he speaks out this knowledge, they drop dead!
- In Acts 5:12 it says that the Apostles performed all kinds of miraculous *signs* and *wonders*.
- In Acts 7 a man named Stephen, said to be full of the Holy Spirit, has the *courage to face martyrdom*.
- In Acts 9:17-18 the Apostle Paul is *healed* of temporary blindness.

And so, we could go on. In Romans 12 and 1 Corinthians 12, we read of the manifestation of the Holy Spirit's power on a person in the form of spiritual *charisma* (gifts). These impart a special ability to perform certain tasks or touch the lives of people, that was not possible or as effective before. They are a direct result of being filled or baptised in Holy Spirit.

The result or the point of being baptised in the Holy Spirit is a special empowering to do the works of the Kingdom, to minister on God's behalf, and to fulfil the functions he has given us. That is why we need to be filled with the Spirit

It is important to note that being filled with the Spirit does not make us mature or righteous or more spiritual than other people. Being baptised in the Spirit is not a rung on the spiritual-maturity-ladder. People can be empowered to do certain tasks, but still be immature and carnal in their personal lives and relationships with other people. Paul's letter to the Corinthians is a good example of that, and many have tripped up on this point. Being baptised in the Holy Spirit has to do with empowering for service, not spiritual maturity or righteousness. The sign of spiritual maturity is better defined as the *fruit* of the Spirit, not the *gifts* or special abilities that we can perform.

The gift of tongues

A major issue of contention that has arisen with respect to teaching on baptism (or being filled) with the Holy Spirit is its relationship to speaking in tongues. For instance, some Christians have asserted categorically that *the* immediate sign of a person being baptised in the Spirit is the ability to speak or pray in an unlearned tongue (i.e. a language unknown to the person speaking it.) Indeed, in some circles, there were even those who taught that if people did not speak in tongues they were not really saved!

Given that there are different views on this, a simple reading of Scripture fails to find any categorical reference to the spiritual gift of tongues as being *the* sign or proof that a person has been filled or baptised with the Holy Spirit. Now, it did happen that way on the Day of Pentecost, and it did happen in *some* of the other instances recorded in the book of Acts where the Holy Spirit came upon people. But there are also other instances in Acts where a person was filled with the Holy Spirit, and there is a notable absence of any record of them speaking in tongues. When the Bible is explicit, we can be dogmatic. But when the Bible is not explicit, maybe we need to be cautious about building our theology around one's own experience. Those who make the Bible out to say what it does not say are just as guilty as those who discredit and dispute what the Bible does actually say!

A simple approach to take is that the gift of tongues is something the Spirit gives whenever, and to whomever, he chooses. It is evidently not universally given or manifested in every believer but in those of the Spirit's choosing. It is certainly not a proof that a person is baptised in the Holy Spirit, for there are many deeply devout Christians who are clearly Spirit-filled and Spirit-gifted, yet they have never spoken in tongues. They may well be open to doing so, and may have even sought it on many occasions, but God has not seen fit to grant that particular gift to them. Instead, he has gifted them in other ways that are equally important and equally evidential of an in-filling type encounter.

Having said that, it perhaps needs to be noted that the ability to pray or speak in tongues does seem to be one of the most common and immediate experiences of those who are prayed over to be filled with the Spirit. This does not happen in every case but in a significant number of occasions. Therefore, we all need to be open to it. In fact, it might even be said that having an objection to speaking in tongues is tantamount to accusing the Holy Spirit of not knowing what he is doing. Some people keen for prayer to be filled with the Spirit add as a caveat or proviso that they do not wish to speak in tongues. That is an unwise position to take, as it is really not for us to decide. God gives the gifts, and we do not choose the ones we want and those we do not. If we want Jesus to baptise us in the Holy Spirit, we need to let him set the agenda of what happens afterward.

What we can be sure of when we are filled with the Spirit is an endowment with power in order to fulfil the mission Jesus has given us. That was the experience of the New Testament believers, and that is what we need today. Those first Christians were miraculously transformed by the Holy Spirit; the same thing needs to . . . and can . . . happen to us!

3. When does baptism in Holy Spirit occur?

At what point should a person be filled with the Spirit? The short answer to that is: *at the point at which they seek it!* When we hunger and thirst after God, he delights in answering. How did Jesus put it?

> [11] *"Which of you fathers, if your son asks for a fish, will give him a snake instead?* [12] *Or if he asks for an egg, will give him a scorpion?* [13] *If you then, though you are evil, know how to give good gifts to your children, how much more will your Father in heaven give the Holy Spirit to those who ask him!"*
>
> Luke 11:11-13

If we follow through the examples in the Book of Acts, we find a variety of occasions when believers were filled with the Holy Spirit. In most cases, however, it was within the context of (or close to) their own conversion. That is arguably God's intention. As soon as we come into a relationship with Jesus we need to be filled with the Holy Spirit.

This is the context for Peter's comment in Acts 2 when people asked him what they had to do to get their lives right with God. In addition to repentance and baptism in water, he talked about receiving the gift of the Holy Spirit. We might say that this is God's ideal, and why in many churches prayer for people who are being baptised in water includes that they may also be baptised in the Holy Spirit. Unfortunately for many believers, the sequence of events in their spiritual journey has not been like that. They have known the Lord and believed in him for a long, long time, but they've never experienced or even wanted the filling of the Holy Spirit.

One of the greatest areas of confusion over baptism in the Holy Spirit has been an assertion by some Bible teachers that it all happens at (or is concurrent with) the point at which a person comes to faith in Christ. When we pray and invite Jesus to become the Lord of our life, the argument goes, baptism in the Holy Spirit happens at that point. We are cleansed of our past sin and forgiven, and we receive the gift of the Holy Spirit (as Peter speaks of it in Acts 2). It all happens at conversion, and baptism in the Holy Spirit is simply a part of the conversion package. If we're describing the concept of conversion to Christianity as a process that takes place over a period of time, maybe there is a place for seeing baptism in the Spirit as part of our conversion. In that sense, it is legitimately a part of the process, along with repentance, water baptism and being added to the Church—all of which are part of the process of change that God does in a person's life. But if we are thinking of conversion as the instant we are mysteriously saved and have our names written in heaven, then there is a parting company with those who assert that it all happens at conversion.

Dr. Martyn Lloyd Jones (the great preacher and former Minister of Westminster Chapel) has a delightful response to those who claim they "get it all" at conversion:

> *Got it all? Well, if you have "got it all" I simply ask, in the name of God why are you as you are? If you have got it all, why are you so unlike the New Testament Christians? Got it all! Got it all at conversion! Well, where is it, I ask?* [14]

What is true to say of our initial conversion experience is that we receive the person of the Holy Spirit. In Chapter Two we noted how Paul, writing to the church in Corinth, referred to the Holy Spirit indwelling Christians. He also wrote in a similar vein to the churches in Rome and Galatia:

> [9] *... if anyone does not have the Spirit of Christ he does not belong to Christ.*
>
> *Romans 8:9*

> [6] *God sends the Spirit of his Son into our hearts . . .*

---

[14] Dr Martyn Lloyd Jones, "Quenching The Spirit", (The Westminster Record, September 1964)

Galatians 4:6

In fact, it might be truer to suggest that the person of the Holy Spirit is present and active in us long before we reach the point of salvation—gradually wooing us and drawing us to faith in Jesus. His activity in our lives might be likened to a spiritual gestation period. But there is all the world of difference between receiving the *person* of the Holy Spirit and being endued with Holy Spirit *power*. In that sense, believing and receiving can be separate events. Sadly, for many Christians, the time in between can be very long indeed. As mentioned in Chapter Two, it is possible to have the mains electricity connected to one's house but never throw the switch to turn it on!

The question may not so much be about receiving the *person* of the Holy Spirit. He is already there. But are we being filled or immersed in the *power* or *nature* of the Holy Spirit? Do we know his power and nature in our lives? Have we been immersed or saturated or filed or anointed or overwhelmed *by* the Holy Spirit?

As Paul says in Ephesians 5:18 that we should not be filled with wine, which leads to debauchery, but instead we should be intoxicated or filled with Holy Spirit. Or as someone poignantly put it: "Is he resident, or is he president?" And we may well contend that it is at that point that so many Christians today are missing out on the fullness of what God has for them. They are going through the right religious motions but never experiencing the dynamic of being empowered by the Holy Spirit.

The Father gave us the Spirit to come alongside us and help us fulfil our calling and mission. The best way he is able to do that is to pour his nature and power into our lives.

Four

How can I be Baptised in the Holy Spirit?

We turn our attention now to how it actually happens. What steps can a person take in order to experience being filled with the Spirit? We have established that there is a difference between receiving the person of the Holy Spirit and being filled or immersed in his power. The person of the Holy Spirit has been present and active in us from the point of our conversion. In fact, before that; he was the one who gently and patiently drew us to faith in Christ in the first place. But the objective of the Holy Spirit is not so much to *reside* in us, as to *preside*. Remember R.A. Torrey's question: *"Do we have more of him, or does he have more of us?"*[15]

In Chapter Three stress was laid on the fact that the Apostle Peter interpreted the Pentecostal experience of being filled with the Spirit as something other Christians could anticipate also. Following on through the Book of Acts, that presupposition of Peter's is consistent with both the teaching and experience of the early Church. Other believers also had an experience or an encounter with the person of the Holy Spirit, whereby they were filled with his power. This appears to have equipped them to minister in the Name of Jesus in a fashion they were not capable of before.

The following selection of passages from the Book of Acts illustrates this. Among other things, note the variety of ways in which it happened:

> [14] *When the apostles in Jerusalem heard that Samaria had accepted the word of God, they sent Peter and John to Samaria.* [15] *When they arrived, they prayed for the new believers there that they might receive the Holy Spirit,* [16] *because the Holy Spirit had not yet come on any of them; they had simply been baptized into the name of the Lord Jesus.* [17] *Then Peter and John placed their hands on them, and they received the Holy Spirit.*
>
> Acts 8:14-17

> [15] *But the Lord said to Ananias, "Go! This man is my chosen instrument to proclaim my name to the Gentiles and their kings and to the people of Israel.* [16] *I will show him how much he must suffer for my name."* [17] *Then Ananias went to the house and entered it. Placing his hands on Saul, he said, "Brother Saul, the Lord—Jesus, who appeared to you on the road as you were coming here—has sent me so that you may see again and be filled with the Holy Spirit."* [18] *Immediately, something like scales fell from Saul's eyes, and he could see again. He got up and was baptized,* [19] *and after taking*

---

[15] David Watson, *"One in the Spirit"*, (Hodder & Stoughton, 1973), p.25

some food, he regained his strength. Saul spent several days with the disciples in Damascus.

Acts 9:15-19

[44] While Peter was still speaking these words, the Holy Spirit came on all who heard the message. [45] The circumcised believers who had come with Peter were astonished that the gift of the Holy Spirit had been poured out even on Gentiles. [46] For they heard them speaking in tongues and praising God. Then Peter said, [47] "Surely no one can stand in the way of their being baptized with water. They have received the Holy Spirit just as we have." [48] So he ordered that they be baptized in the name of Jesus Christ. Then they asked Peter to stay with them for a few days.

Acts 10:44-48

[1] While Apollos was at Corinth, Paul took the road through the interior and arrived at Ephesus. There he found some disciples [2] and asked them, "Did you receive the Holy Spirit when you believed?" They answered, "No, we have not even heard that there is a Holy Spirit."

[3] So Paul asked, "Then what baptism did you receive?"

"John's baptism," they replied.

[4] Paul said, "John's baptism was a baptism of repentance. He told the people to believe in the one coming after him, that is, in Jesus." [5] On hearing this, they were baptized into the name of the Lord Jesus. [6] When Paul placed his hands on them, the Holy Spirit came on them, and they spoke in tongues and prophesied. [7] There were about twelve men in all.

Acts 19:1-7

At the risk of labouring an illustration, when we come to faith in Christ, it is like having the mains electricity connected to our house. When we are baptised in the Spirit, it is like throwing the switch and having current flowing through all the wiring. For many believers, the mains electricity is connected but the switch has never been turned on.

Well, how does it happen? What do we actually do in order to experience being filled or baptised in Holy Spirit? By way of introduction let's deal with three common misconceptions about what happens when we are filled with the Spirit:

Misconception No. 1: Baptism in the Holy Spirit is synonymous with sanctification

The word sanctification has to do with holiness. It describes the process of being separated from the evil things in our world, unto the Lord. Sanctification or spiritual maturity is to be the goal of every Christian. Once we are saved by God from the clutches and consequences of our sin it is the aim of every believer to become more sanctified or spiritually mature. We endeavour to be less like the people of this world and more like Jesus.

There are some Christians who speak as if baptism in the Holy Spirit is a means or a short-cut toward becoming more spiritually mature. That it is a misconception of both the experience of, and the motive for, being filled with the Spirit. Unfortunately, this misconception has done considerable damage and has contributed to the development of a theology that totally rejects teaching on baptism in the Holy Spirit.

A lot of the confusion arises from testimonies or boasting that people give after an experience of being filled with the Spirit. They have been touched by God in a dramatic way, and in their enthusiasm and desire to give God the glory, they testify that baptism in the Spirit saved their marriage, or gave them victory over sin, or helped them beat destructive habits like smoking or drug abuse. They tell how they have lived a much more "holy" life since they were filled with the Spirit.

However, in many cases, when you listen to their language and conversation outside of a church context, or watch the way they speak to their spouse, or observe their attitudes toward employers, or note the way they pay their bills, the level of their spiritual maturity or sanctification seems largely unaffected by their experience. They are just as carnal and unholy and unsanctified as those who have not had their experience. Many people have heard testimonies along these lines and it has put them off. Baptism in the Spirit appears to be worn as a kind of spiritual merit badge. They boldly ask others, *"Have you had the baptism brother . . . have you got the gift of tongues yet?"* As if to say: "Are you in the club?" The impression is given that being filled with the Spirit is a means of growing up into spiritual maturity. The sad conclusion that many have drawn goes like this: *"Because of their inconsistency and lack of basic spiritual maturity, the experience of the Holy Spirit that they boast of must have been counterfeit or mere emotional hype. Therefore, I can reject their testimony and their teaching on baptism in the Holy Spirit."*

That is an unfortunate conclusion to draw. Nowhere in the New Testament is sanctification or spiritual maturity laid down as either a prerequisite for, or a direct result of having been, filled with the Holy Spirit. There is no statement in the Scriptures that says we must have rooted out and overcome all our sinful habits before we can be baptised in the Spirit. Nor does it ever say that as a result of such an empowering experience spiritual maturity will result. Some people have implied that baptism in water and baptism in the Spirit are for those believers who have got their act together. As if once a person has fully perfected their repentance, then they can be filled with the Spirit. The example of the New Testament is quite to the contrary. Both baptism in water and the Holy Spirit, according to the Book of Acts, tended to happen right at the beginning of the conversion process of new believers, not sometime later once they had proven themselves.

Baptism in the Holy Spirit means an empowering for ministry, not a sign or symbol of spiritual maturity. Perhaps a sound Biblical example of this might be the book of 1 Corinthians. Here was a group of people baptised in the Spirit and operating in all the spiritual *charisma*, but whose fundamental Christian maturity and sanctification was woefully lacking. They could prophesy and speak in tongues, heal the sick and cast out demons; but at the same time slander their brothers and sister, and spread vile rumours against their leaders—even tolerate sexual perversion and immorality within the church.

No, to be filled with the Spirit does not imply either that you have to be spiritually mature before the event, or that you will be spiritually mature after the event. What is true to say of those who are filled with the Spirit is that they have a desire or a thirst to be clean vessels for God's use. According to the teaching of Jesus, the prerequisite condition for receiving the empowering of the Holy Spirit (John 7:37-39) is thirst, and the result (Acts 1:8) is power in order to be his witnesses. The process of sanctification does not have to be, and will not be, completed simply because we are filled with the Spirit.

An illustration might help us understand this. Take a jug that we wish to fill with water. The point at which water overflows the rim of the jug is when we may say it is full—no more water can get in. If that jug is already half filled with rocks, to begin with, it is still possible for it to be filled to overflowing. However, if those rocks are removed, it is possible for more water to enter the jug. Let's be honest, we all still have a few rocks in our jug! They should not be there; they are taking up room that should be occupied by the activity of the Holy Spirit. He is working on us day by day so that they might be removed and more of him can enter. But praise God: even with a few rocks in the jug, we can still know what it means to be filled.

According to Paul in Romans 15:16 and 2 Thessalonians 2:13, the Holy Spirit is constantly at work within us, sanctifying us and helping us grow up into spiritual maturity. But it is quite wrong for us to confuse the experience of being baptised in the Spirit (empowered for ministry) as a sign or proof that the process of sanctification has been completed.

Misconception No. 2: Baptism in the Holy Spirit is a once-only event

A common error in the testimony of many Christians is to talk of baptism in the Spirit in the same way as they talk of their conversion to Christ; looking back to the day when they "got it", or when it "happened" to them. Praise God for the experience such testimonies are describing, but better to hear a testimony of an *ongoing* experience of being filled with the Spirit, rather than just the initiation.

Baptism in or being filled with the person and power of the Holy Spirit, according to the New Testament, does not merely describe an initiation type experience, but also a repetitive and a continual state. It is not so much to be viewed as an event that we can look back to, as we can with water baptism, but rather as a perpetual or repetitive encounter that we are called to have with the Holy Spirit.

This is demonstrated in a number of places in the Book of Acts. In Acts 2:4, on the Day of Pentecost, it says of those first believers that:

> All of them were filled with the Holy Spirit . . .

That was their initiation experience. But if we roll forward a couple of chapters, into Acts 4:31, we read these words:

> After they prayed, the place where they were meeting was shaken. And they were all filled with the Holy Spirit and spoke the word of God boldly.

If we get filled with the Spirit only once, and that is it, then how come these first Christians were all filled a second time? Then there is Paul's experience. In Acts 9:17-18 Ananias laid his hands upon Paul and he was filled with the Spirit. But then in Acts 13:9 it seems he was filled again in order to minister.

The great revivalist preacher, D.L. Moody was once asked if he was filled with the Spirit. Moody is said to have responded: "Yes I am . . . but I leak!" If all there is of the Spirit's fullness is what we got some years back, then we have cause to feel cheated. We had our "bit" and it has drained out! But that is obviously not how the Apostle Paul saw it when he wrote his letter to the Ephesians. In Ephesians 5:18 we read these words:

> Do not get drunk on wine, which leads to debauchery. Instead, be filled with the Spirit.

If we go back to the original Greek for this verse, the verb *be filled* is in the present continuous tense. It describes something that continues happening, rather than something that happens just once. A better translation would be: *". . . go on continually being filled with the Holy Spirit."* We need to see baptism in the Holy Spirit as more than just an initial event that happened to us at one time in our spiritual journey. We may well look back to when this relationship began, but if we have not prayed for it to be renewed since, chances are we need to. If you were asked the question: *"When were you baptised in the Holy Spirit?"* the correct response ought to be, *"Which time do you mean?"* The rocks that are still in our jug mean that the power of the Holy Spirit drains out of us. We need to come back repeatedly to the fountain and have another drink.

Maybe that is something that the Lord is asking of us as we read this book. Perhaps we can look back to a time in our past when we sought prayer to be filled with the Spirit. The Lord met us there, and we were touched by him in a dynamic way. Is he asking us to come back to the fountain, to be filled again? There is no shame in that. This side of our heavenly home D.L. Moody's experience is common to us all: *we leak!* If it means we can better serve Jesus, we want to come back to the fountain again and again.

Misconception No. 3: Baptism in the Holy Spirit results in frenzied emotionalism

A group of pastors in a particular city were once surveyed as to why so little emphasis was given in their preaching and teaching to the ministry and work of the Holy Spirit. The most consistent response went something like: *"We're afraid that our people would be led into emotionalism and fanaticism, and that it would cause splits and irreparable damage to the church."* So, out of self-preservation, they avoided the subject. Many pastors and churches have shied away from the subject; better not to rock the boat, not to be controversial. No doubt the devil has a wonderful time laughing at the fear and division he causes, stopping disciples of Jesus from discovering all God has for them.

The point needs to be made very firmly: The Holy Spirit is not in the business of making fools or fanatics out of *anyone!* He is the Holy Spirit. He is a gentleman, and he can be trusted. Just because some men and women have made a fool of themselves does not necessarily mean that the Holy Spirit has caused it. The devil delights in causing distortions of truth and imbalanced excesses, or counterfeits of genuine experience. We need to learn to rest in the faithfulness of God and yield to him to do with us whatever he wants. He does not make a fool of us or embarrass us.

If we have hesitation about seeking prayer to be filled with the Spirit, maybe we need to ask ourselves another question: Is Jesus really Lord? It is one thing to wade into the river of life, keeping our feet firmly planted on the sandy bottom. It is another thing to take our feet off the bottom, and float, letting the Spirit of God take us wherever he wants. That word "yield" is a key verb in describing what it means to be filled with the Spirit.

How does it happen?

What exactly do we do in order to be baptised or filled with the Holy Spirit? Firstly, and perhaps most obviously, the experience of being filled with the Spirit comes in response to prayer. We ask God to do it. Jesus is the one, according to John the Baptist, who baptizes us in the Holy Spirit. So, if we want it to happen to us, surely the best place to start is by asking Jesus to do it. It is something we can request of him with the full confidence that it is in accordance with his will.

Secondly, if we note the occasions in the Book of Acts where people were filled with the Spirit, the most consistent manner was via the laying on of hands by a mature brother or sister in the Lord:

> Acts 8:17 - *"Peter and John placed their hands on them, and they received the Holy Spirit."*
> Acts 9:17 - *"Placing his hands on Saul, he said…be filled with the Holy Spirit."*
> Acts 19:6 - *"When Paul placed his hands on them the Holy Spirit came on them."*

As hands were laid on them symbolising the touch of God the

power of the Spirit was released into the people being prayed for. That was also my own experience. There was a time as a teenager when the Lord had been provoking me about being filled with the Spirit. In the end, I sought the counsel of someone I trusted, and he laid his hands on me and prayed.

But the point needs to be made that having someone lay hands on us is not the only way to be baptised in, or filled with, the Holy Spirit. In Acts 2, on the Day of Pentecost, it simply says that:

> ... *they were all together in one place.* ^{2} *Suddenly a sound like the blowing of a violent wind came from heaven and filled the whole house where they were sitting.* ^{3} *They saw what seemed to be tongues of fire that separated and came to rest on each of them.* ^{4} *All of them were filled with the Holy Spirit ...*
>
> Acts 2:1-4

Likewise, in Acts 10:44-48, when Peter was preaching to Cornelius and his household the text says:

> ... *while Peter was still speaking these words, the Holy Spirit came on all who heard the message ...*

There was no one there laying hands on people. God just did it, sovereignly.

If Jesus' experience is anything of an example to us, the Holy Spirit came upon him in the form of a descending dove at the time of his baptism in water. In fact, in just about every case in Acts where people were filled with the Spirit, they were also baptised in water either immediately before it or immediately afterward. When we read through the testimonies of some of the great men and women of God in Church history, we again find a variety of occasions and situations. For men like Hudson Taylor, Charles Finney, and D.L. Moody it happened while they were alone with the Lord. For Hudson Taylor, it happened on 4th

September 1869 while on a personal retreat at the little mission station in Chin Kiang. For Charles Finney, it was in the back room of a County Law Office. He had an encounter with the Holy Spirit that lasted the whole night long. For Moody, it was something he had been seeking for some time, and it happened to him while walking down, of all places, Wall St in New York City.

The nature of the experience may differ from person to person. What God does with you will be quite different from what or how he does it with someone else. It is Jesus who administers baptism in the Holy Spirit, and how he chooses to do so is fundamentally his choice. In fact, it is probably the case that some people have been genuinely and unmistakably filled with the Spirit without ever consciously asking. It is simply something God, in his sovereignty, has done to them. As mentioned above, my personal experience was one of seeking and wrestling with God, and finally asking someone to pray with me. That is the experience of many others. But others have simply shut themselves away in their prayer closet, alone with the Lord, and He has met them and filled them. No one else was present.

The nature of the experience is different, but the fundamental question is the same: Are we filled with the Spirit? If we do not know for sure, what stops us from asking? And if we know for certain that God did touch us and release his power through us in the past, what stops us from coming back to the fountain again for another drink? The Father-God revealed in the Bible turns no one away who comes to him asking to be filled (or refilled) with the Holy Spirit. It is something he delights to do that we might be empowered to better fulfil the assignment he has given us.

In conclusion:

Maybe you're at the stage where you genuinely seek to be baptised or filled with Holy Spirit? The following are a series of propositions or challenges based on a number of New Testament passages that refer to receiving Holy Spirit. They are four conditions of the heart that might be viewed as a prerequisite to baptism in the Holy Spirit.

1. Repentance & Baptism

As noted on a number of occasions Peter, on the Day of Pentecost, spoke of the gift of the Holy Spirit for all whom the Lord our God would call. But note again the context of that gift:

> [38] . . . *Repent and be baptised, every one of you, in the name of Jesus Christ for the forgiveness of sins. And you will receive the gift of the Holy Spirit.*
>
> Acts 2:38

We can turn this statement around: *"You'll receive the gift of the Holy Spirit when you have repented and been baptised . . ."* Have we made a ruthless break with our past life where we were the boss? Repentance, by definition, means turning our back on our sinful past. As best we are able, it means setting to right relationships that were broken, and turning our lives over to Jesus and his Lordship. Have we been prepared to make a public declaration of our faith in Jesus? As we noted in Chapter one, the act of baptism stands for just that; death to our old life, and resurrection to a new life where Jesus is Lord. We do not have to be perfect before God fills us with his Spirit, but the attitude of our heart or our desire needs to be pure.

2. Obedience

In Acts 5 the Apostles were brought before the Sanhedrin and grilled because of their persistence in preaching about Jesus. This is one of the comments Peter made in their defence:

> [32] *We are witnesses of these things, and so is the Holy Spirit, whom God has given to those who obey him.*
>
> Acts 5:32

Who did Peter say the Holy Spirit is given to? Those who are obedient to the Lord. Jesus said something similar in John 14:21:

> *Whoever has my commands and keeps them is the one who loves me. Anyone who loves me will be loved by my Father, and I too will love them and show myself to him*

The person to whom the Lord reveals himself is obedient to the commands God has given. Obedience is a demonstration of love for God. The Holy Spirit is given to those who walk in obedience to what the Lord is asking. Those who tarry or disobey will not be filled with the Spirit. A request to be filled with the Spirit is an act of submission and yielding; a statement that we are prepared to receive from God whatever he wants us to receive, and to go wherever he wants us to go. Being filled with Holy Spirit implies being emptied of ourselves and our selfish ambitions. In seeking to be filled, are we willing to obey whatever the Lord asks of us?

3. Thirst

In John 7 we read these words of Jesus:

> [37] On the last and greatest day of the Festival, Jesus stood and said in a loud voice, "Let anyone who is thirsty come to me and drink. [38] Whoever believes in me, as Scripture has said, rivers of living water will flow from within them." [39] By this he meant the Spirit, whom those who believed in him were later to receive. Up to that time the Spirit had not been given, since Jesus had not yet been glorified.
>
> John 7:37-39

Is there a longing, a thirsting within us for all that God has for us? If ever there was a prerequisite condition in the life of a believer for the in-filling of the Holy Spirit, this is it: a searching and a wrestling after the things of God. Jesus also said:

> [6] Blessed are those who hunger and thirst for righteousness, for they will be filled.
>
> Matthew 5:6

If we have a deep longing for more of God, we will be satisfied. God will meet us.

4. Ask

According to Jesus, those who desire to be filled with Holy Spirit have simply to ask:

> [9] "So I say to you: Ask and it will be given to you; seek and you will find; knock and the door will be opened to you. [10] For everyone who asks receives; those who seek find; and to those who knock, the door will be opened. [11] "Which of you fathers, if your son asks for a fish, will give him a snake instead? [12] Or if he asks for an egg, will give him a scorpion? [13] If you then, though you are evil, know how to give good gifts to your children, how much more will your Father in heaven give the Holy Spirit to those who ask him!"
>
> Luke 11:9-13

There is the promise! All we have to do is ask. Being filled with Holy Spirit is something God wants for us. When we ask it of him, we can be absolutely confident that he will only give what is good. Are we willing to ask?

The late David Watson, in his book, *"One in the Spirit"* offered the following advice to those eager to experience a touch from the Spirit. As a summary statement it cannot be bettered:

> *"Never worry unduly about the precise nature of the experience. Leave that to God. Some experiences of the Spirit's fullness may seem sudden and dramatic; others gradual and gentle. The important thing is to believe that God means what he says. Go out trusting in the Holy Spirit to use you to glorify Jesus. Go on day by day being filled with the Spirit. Watch out for the spiritual battle, which may well be more real than ever. Use the promised power especially to witness to Jesus.* [16]

---

[16] David Watson, *"One In The Spirit"*, (Hodder & Stoughton, 1973), p.20.

www.ingramcontent.com/pod-product-compliance
Lightning Source LLC
Chambersburg PA
CBHW051408290426
44108CB00015B/2208